ANSWERS TO ADD

ATTENTION DEFICIT DISORDER WITH OR WITHOUT HYPERACTIVITY

A PRACTICAL GUIDE FOR PARENTS

A FAMILY POWER SERIES BOOK

by
John F. Taylor, Ph.D.

Illustrated by
Kurt Deppenschmidt

Published by

A.D.D. Plus

488 Glacier Way S.
Monmouth, Oregon 97361
1-800-VIP-1-ADD

www.ADD-Plus.com

2010

CONTENTS

INTRODUCTION

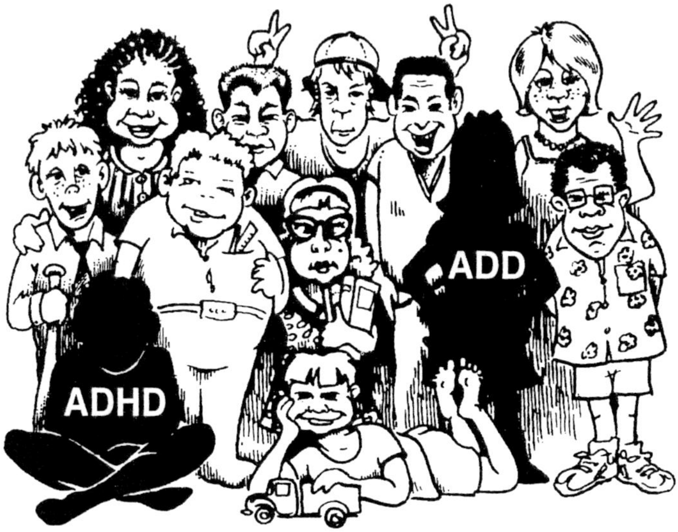

The name for this disorder changes every so often. For easy reading, this booklet uses the term Attention Deficit/Hyperactivity Disorder, abbreviated ADHD, and will use the term *child* to refer to both children and teens.

DEFINITION OF THIS DISORDER:

About 6% of the general population has ADHD, with most being of the "hyperactive-impulsive" type. Those without hyperactivity but with attention-focusing problems are said to have ADHD "inattentive" type. Most children with ADHD are boys. Among Caucasians with ADHD, about half are fair-featured (blue eyes plus blond or red hair). Here are some common signs of this condition. The exact number of signs differs from child to child.

MENTAL TRAITS:

- **DISTRACTIBILITY:** short attention span, bothered by sights and sounds, difficulty concentrating on or finishing tasks, annoyance with boring tasks

- **CONFUSION:** poor goal planning, weak follow-through, forgetfulness, disorganization, tendency to lose things, absent-mindedness

- **CONCRETE THINKING:** trouble with math and logic, inability to see how two things are alike, inability to summarize, trouble using skills in a new situation, need for routines

- **RIGID THINKING:** not flexible, bullheaded, bothered by changes in routine or shifting from one activity to another

- **WEAK LANGUAGE:** stutters, can't find words to say, has trouble reading, seems not to understand when spoken to

- **AIMLESSNESS:** unpredictable, doesn't learn from past mistakes, makes careless errors, poor at planning, poor at resisting temptations

- **WEAK PERCEPTION:** puts on clothing upside down/inside out, reading problems, left-right problems

- **WEAK BODY-AWARENESS:** can't sense passage of time, not aware of hunger or pain, has bowel and bladder accidents, trouble with bonding and friendships

PHYSICAL TRAITS:

- **CONSTANT MOVEMENT:** can't sit still, fidgets, squirms, often moves a body part, runs ahead of companions in public, pokes and grabs, picks at scabs, chatters noisily

- **ABNORMAL DEVELOPMENT:** says first word or takes step before the ninth month or after the fifteenth month

- **FOOD CRAVINGS/AVERSIONS:** fussy eater or craves foods (most common cravings: highly seasoned foods, cheese, sugar)

- **ALLERGIES/SENSITIVITIES:** skin problems, pollen-related allergies, sensitivities (most common: chemicals, pets, medicines, dust, mold, food)

- **SLEEP PROBLEMS:** can't get to sleep, sleeptalks, sleepwalks, sweats excessively, grinds teeth, wakes up screaming, moves restlessly, irritable and disorganized when awakened in morning

- **COORDINATION PROBLEMS:** trouble with balance, jumping rope, handwriting or drawing, athletics

EMOTIONAL TRAITS:

- **SELF-CENTEREDNESS:** can't accept blame, surprised that others are upset, bossy or demanding, invites power struggles, can't attract or hold friends, selfish

- **IMPATIENCE:** hard to please, can't wait in lines, insists on being first in games, badgers and pesters

- **RECKLESSNESS:** breaks things, takes no caution with danger, takes things apart, wears out clothing fast

- **EXTREME EMOTIONS:** very angry or very loving, moody, unpredictable, can't take teasing, is easily frustrated, has anger-control problems

- **WEAK CONSCIENCE:** steals, gets into siblings' rooms, gets talked into mischief, interrupts others, unaware of others' boundaries

No checklist can substitute for a thorough evaluation, but a checklist can be an important help in finding out if a person has ADHD. Pages 28-29 contain a useful checklist for recognizing ADHD in children, teens, and adults. Checklists are also available in Spanish language form, free of charge from A.D.D. Plus. 1-800-VIP-1-ADD.

SIGNS AND INDICATORS AT VARIOUS AGES

Though these signs also occur in non-ADHD children, they often reflect ADHD. There are also many positive traits in ADHD children and each child shows a unique collection of traits.

- **PRENATAL:** hyperactivity (excessive movement)
- **BIRTH:** medical emergencies and stresses, such as breech presentation, high-forceps delivery, oxygen loss
- **INFANCY:** colic, climbing out of or destroying the crib, early or late development of walking and talking, many ear infections
- **TODDLERHOOD/PRESCHOOL:** Five traits that spell the code **RADIO:**

  R: **RECKLESS:** climbs and runs too far, careless with dangers, requires constant supervision, has accidents
  A: **AGGRESSIVE:** can't play well with other toddlers
  D: **DESTRUCTIVE:** breaks toys during rough play or tantrums or by taking things apart
  I: **INCORRIGIBLE:** won't respond to correction or discipline, "terrible twos"
  O: **OVERACTIVE:** fidgets, flits and runs, chatterbox

- **MIDDLE CHILDHOOD:** self-esteem and peer problems worsen, 80% have a school-related problem of some sort, misbehavior and discipline issues worsen, language-related problems show up
- **ADOLESCENCE:** at risk for substance abuse and school problems, power struggles and sneaky misbehavior, attracts peers who are also in trouble, has trouble with academics and career choices

CAUSES OF ADHD

Recent research identifies brain-nerve structure and chemistry problems as the main causes of ADHD. Many aspects of brain chemistry are involved. There is a shortage of key chemicals used by brain nerve cells to send their messages to each other: dopamine (DOPE-ih-meen), norepinephrine (nor-ep-ih-NEF-rin), and serotonin (seh-ruh-TONE-in). These chemicals are made from amino acids, so ADHD can be considered a protein chemistry problem. Also, the brain doesn't conduct its chemical reactions quickly enough—the nerve cells are performing too slowly. If the ADHD brain were an engine, its idling speed would be set too low.

Life stresses such as divorce, child abuse, or malnutrition can cause many ADHD symptoms to appear, even though the child might not have the disorder.

FOUR WAYS TO HELP THE ADHD CHILD

Research shows us that the more methods we use to help the ADHD child, the better. There are four major tool kits:

- **BIOCHEMICAL:** helping the brain nerve cells become stronger, make more of the needed chemicals, and increase the speed of chemical activity
- **SENSORIMOTOR:** working through senses of vision, touch, EEG biofeedback, and related avenues to improve the control of muscle movements, decrease touch defensiveness, and improve perception
- **ACADEMIC:** using special teaching methods to help the student stay motivated and interested in school and to increase understanding and memory of the material being taught
- **PSYCHOLOGICAL:** helping the child and family with self-esteem, improving child discipline, teaching anger-control and other social skills, reducing sibling rivalry

TOOLS FROM THE BIOCHEMICAL TOOL KIT

There is still considerable controversy and disagreement among authorities in this field about biochemical methods. The most famous tool is prescribed medication, mostly stimulants and antidepressants. Research has shown other methods to be helpful, such as eliminating substances to which the child is allergic or sensitive, and increasing proteins. Good nutrition for the child's brain and body is probably also helpful (vitamins, minerals, amino acids, essential fatty acids). Substances that decrease allergic reactions and prevent free-radical damage, such as antioxidant vitamins (beta-carotene, Vitamin C, Vitamin E) and bioflavanoid antioxidants are probably also helpful. Hopefully the current outpouring of research on the usefulness of such nutrients will help clarify their proper role with ADHD.

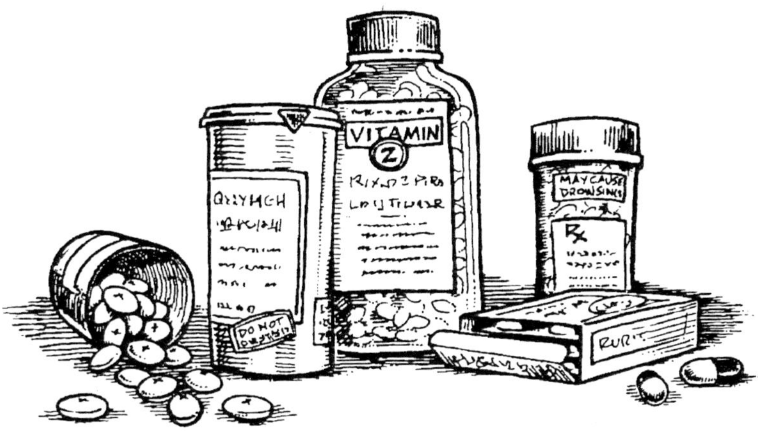

PRESCRIBED MEDICATION:

This method has about a 75% success rate, as judged by parents, when the child is over the age of five. At any given time about 1/3 of ADHD children are taking prescribed medication, and 3/4 will do so some time during their lives. The most common problem is that the dosage level (the size of the pill) is not correct. One way to help your physician understand your child's reaction to the prescription is to send *The Taylor School Medication Effectiveness Report Form* (see pages 30-31) to the physician weekly to determine whether it is necessary to adjust the dosage.

PREVENTING ALLERGIC REACTIONS:

The majority of ADHD children who are having any kind of allergy reaction also tend to show more ADHD symptoms at the same time. Common foods that seem to trigger flare-ups of ADHD symptoms are: cow's milk, corn, wheat, chocolate, sugar, eggs, nuts, oranges, and soy. Allergies to irritants such as dust, pollen, or animal dander can also make ADHD symptoms worse. The research indicates that a significant percentage of ADHD children have some sort of allergy ADHD connection.

The preferred treatment method is to find what the child is reacting to and stop exposing the child to that substance. With a food allergy, for example, the child would stop eating the offending food. Advocates of this method say that it applies at all age levels, from infancy through adult.

PREVENTING SENSITIVITY REACTIONS:

Allergies involve the immune system's attempt to reject a foreign substance, usually creating swelling or red areas of skin. Sensitivities, sometimes called delayed or hidden allergies, have no such signs, but seem to involve the brain's allowing a toxic chemical to disrupt its functions. When an ADHD child has a sensitivity reaction, ADHD symptoms are likely to become worse.

The most common triggers of ADHD symptoms by sensitivity are a group of chemicals called gallic phenols. Many of them are derived from coal or petroleum, and many are lightweight molecules that float up into the air and can be smelled. Examples include paint, varnish, shellac, glue, floor coating, formaldehyde from new carpeting, swimming pool chemicals, dry erase marker odor, and smoke.

Examples of swallowed phenols include petroleum-based food dyes (commonly known as food coloring), artificial flavorings, preservatives (BHA, BHT, TBHQ), and the flavor enhancer MSG. Advocates of this method say that the artificial sweetener aspartame is also troublesome, as are certain fruits that contain a naturally occurring substance that reacts in the same way as the man-made phenols.

This method involves controlling what the child breathes and eats. Shopping is done in ordinary food markets, but careful label reading is needed. Any parent interested in using this method can obtain helpful guidelines from a national support organization. Materials include a state-by-state grocery shopping guide that lists by brand name the foods that are additive-free. *

INCREASING PROTEINS:

The brain makes dopamine and norepinephrine from amino acids. Putting more amino acids into the bloodstream seems to help reduce ADHD symptoms, probably by making the building blocks for these needed chemicals more available.

Include a protein-rich food source in every meal and every snack. Plant sources include tofu, whole grains, nuts, seeds, peas, beans, and soy-based protein powder. Animal sources include unflavored gelatin, red meat, white meat, dairy products, eggs, milk-based protein powder, and fish. Advocates of this method advise avoiding empty-calorie meals, or at least accompanying high-sugar food with a protein-rich food.

PROVIDING GOOD NUTRITION:

For proper function, brain nerve cells require vitamins, minerals, amino acids, and essential fatty acids. There has recently been increased research on the use of these substances to reduce ADHD symptoms. Advocates of this method point out that a diet high in cholesterol, fat, sugar, and phenols can't be expected to help nerve cells very much.

* These methods are controversial, and many authorities on ADHD disagree about their merits. For complete details on how to use this method, see *Helping Your Hyperactive ADD Child,* available from A.D.D. Plus.

TOOLS FROM THE SENSORIMOTOR TOOL KIT

Techniques for assisting sensory and muscle systems are the subject of great debate in the field of ADHD. Most have only a limited amount of scientific research behind them.

EYE-MOVEMENT THERAPY:

This treatment, provided by optometrists, involves training the eye muscles. The goals include decreased visual distractibility and creating smoother eye movement from left to right as the child reads.

AUDITORY TRAINING:

Recently introduced from France, this method involves equalizing the sensitivity of the child's ears so that neither ear is favored. The result, according to advocates of this method, is reduced auditory distractibility.

SENSORY-INTEGRATION THERAPY:

Developed by occupational therapists, this method involves an array of interventions centering on skin and balance. The results, according to its advocates, include decreases in touch sensitivity, fidgeting, and distractibility.

COLORED LENSES:

Visual perception can sometimes be improved if the child looks through special colored lenses. Variations of this tool include providing the child's schoolwork on tinted paper rather than white paper and having the child wear slightly tinted sunglasses.

NEUROFEEDBACK:

Of the tools in the sensorimotor tool kit, this one has the greatest amount of research backing it. The child performs ordinary activities while connected to a computer recording a painless EEG. After several sessions (average treatment involves 50 to 60 sessions), changes in beta and theta wave activity, learned by the process of biofeedback, result in a decrease in many ADHD symptoms.

TOOLS FROM THE ACADEMIC TOOL KIT

There is great overlap between students with learning disabilities and those with ADHD. About 80% of ADHD students have some sort of academic problem, and about 50% are estimated to be underachieving at school. Their most common complaint about school is that they can't keep up with the work load. On the other hand, ADHD seems to be related to IQ level, and many ADHD students are candidates for gifted and talented programs.

BECOME AN ALLY:

Keep a notebook of your child's school history. Include grade reports, samples of work, notes from phone calls and talks with teachers, copies of test results, guidelines for special education and legal rights of students, names and addresses of support groups, school-year calendar, and related information. You can refer to it for suggestions about what other teachers have found helpful for your child.

Maintain communication through phone and personal contact, notes, and forms such as *The Taylor Classroom Daily Report Form* (page 32).

Be clear in stating your concerns and use a friendly tone of voice. Talk with the teacher near the start of the school year. After every conference or phone call, send the teacher a letter summarizing what was agreed on.

If possible, become a source of help for the teacher and volunteer as an aide. Offer tapes, books, magazines articles, and booklets on classroom techniques helpful for ADHD students.*

---

* Dr. Taylor's comprehensive video *Answers to A.D.D.: The School Success Tool Kit* and companion manual *The Attention Deficit/Hyperactive Student at School* are excellent for this purpose. Both are available from A.D.D. Plus.

HIGHLIGHT YOUR CHILD'S NEEDS:

Help your child's teachers find ways to make the learning experience successful for your child. Also be sensitive to the needs of the teacher and the other students. You're not trying to be overprotective, but you do know what's best for your child. Encourage methods that take advantage of your child's strengths. Federal laws prohibit schools from using teaching methods that highlight the weaknesses or learning difficulties of ADHD students. Teachers are required to use all possible "reasonable accommodations" in the regular classroom setting whenever an ADHD student has an academic, social, or learning problem.

ORGANIZE YOUR CHILD'S NOTEBOOK:

Collections of folders or notebooks with many pockets are not good. Follow these guidelines for your child's notebook, and renew it weekly to keep it organized:

- Use a standard three-ring notebook.
- Place a brightly colored weekly assignment sheet inside the front cover.
- Use a paper punch designed for 3-ring notebooks, so your child can punch and insert materials given out by the teacher.
- Give your child a zipper pouch containing helpful items such as ruler, eraser, extra pens and pencils, tissues, sharpener, lunch ticket, and protein snack (peanuts, string cheese, etc.).
- Use laminated study guides and key information such as commonly misspelled words, weights and measures, and times tables.
- Use color-coded dividers *without* pockets.
- Put fresh paper behind every divider.
- Use a sheet protector for storing homework that has been done. Place it at the rear of the notebook.

PROVIDE A GOOD BREAKFAST:

Send your child to school ready to think clearly. Avoid empty-calorie, sugary or pure-carbohydrate breakfasts. Provide a substantial protein-rich meal including whole grains, seeds, soy-based or milk-based protein powder, milk, meat, cheese, yogurt, egg, nut products, or fish, for example. Of course, avoid any foods to which the child seems to have an allergic reaction.

MAKE LEARNING AN ADVENTURE:

Encourage play that has a learning component. Read with your child and point out educational aspects of whatever your child experiences. Attend educational programs with your child. Encourage the use of encyclopedias and a home computer. Most students with ADHD enjoy learning on computers. Use mealtime to discuss what your child is learning at school. Emphasize the process of learning and exploring, rather than the end product of high grades.

ENCOURAGE WISE CLASSROOM HABITS:

Tape recording or taking good notes are essential for success in the classroom. To make studying easier, tell your child to take notes on only one side of each page. Teach the 5 L's of good listening and note-taking:

- **LOCATE** yourself near the teacher. Sit in the front row or in the front cluster of desks.
- **LOOK** at the teacher's eyes. When the teacher looks away from you, look through the teacher's head to where the eyes would be.
- **LINES** should divide topics. Draw lines across your notepaper whenever the teacher changes the topic. Don't try to outline your notes.
- **LIMIT** the use of words. Use symbols and abbreviations as much as possible.

- ▶ **LISTEN** for test items. Don't try to write down everything; just note future test questions from the teacher's lecture. You can spot them with **BROIL**. Make written notes if the teacher:

  B: Writes something on the **BOARD**.
  R: **REPEATS** something.
  O: Says something will be **ON THE NEXT TEST.**
  I: Says something is **IMPORTANT**.
  L: Gives a **LIST**; mentions two or more of anything.

PREVENT HOMEWORK HASSLES:

Sometimes students with ADHD spend so much time on homework that their evenings and weekends are ruined. If your child is spending more than two hours nightly in high school, 90 minutes per night in middle school or junior high, and 45 minutes nightly in elementary school, something is wrong. The best time for homework is between 3:00 and 6:00 P.M., after a half-hour break which includes a protein-rich snack.

Establish a quiet, well-lit place with a straight-back chair and an uncluttered desk. Protect against noises or interruptions. Some sort of white noise is helpful, such as an air conditioner, fan, aquarium aerator, music, or air purifier. Provide a dishpan-sized bin to hold paper, pencils, pens, erasers, rulers, dictionary, a huge supply of 3" x 5" or 4" x 6" note cards, and other necessary materials.

Tell your child to do the hard items last. A good guide is, "If you can't solve it in two minutes, drop it. Move on to the next item, then retry the difficult item later."

To help form good homework habits, have your child use a stopwatch to measure true study time. Your child is to stop the watch whenever there is any interruption (staring out the window, using the bathroom, getting a drink of water, talking to someone). The goal is to have a certain amount of true study time per afternoon or evening. Allow 20% break times, so that there would be a 5-minute break after 25 minutes of true study time, for example.

Have your child make a *School Success Calendar* for long-term assignments and upcoming tests. Start with a rule of 15 minutes of study per afternoon for each item on the calendar.

INSURE SUCCESS ON TESTS:

The best procedure for ADHD students is to transfer lecture notes to note cards, with a likely test question on one side of the card and the answer on the other side. Good class notes consist of nothing but test question after test question, so your child can easily make the cards from his/her lecture notes.

Listed items are generally hard for ADHD students to memorize. Help your child invent a code, using the first letters of the words of the list. Suppose, for example, your child must memorize the five Great Lakes: Erie, Ontario, Superior, Michigan, and Huron. The first letters are E, O, S, M, and H. Help your child think of a way to hook those letters together—either by spelling a word with them (H-O-M-E-S spells "homes") or by making a sentence using the same first letters (Super Man Helps Every One). The code goes on one side of a list-code card, and the answer (the list) goes on the other. For every list there are two cards, a question-and-answer card and a list-code card. Self-quizzing with the cards is the best way to study. You can assist from time to time, and allow reverse quizzing, so that you provide the answer and your child tells you the question. List questions and list-code cards are best memorized by having your child pace the floor or ride a stationary bike while reciting both sides of the cards aloud.

Encourage your child to review lists and list codes immediately prior to taking the test. Of course, provide a substantial breakfast on the morning of the test and make sure your child gets a good night's sleep the night before.

TOOLS FROM THE PSYCHOLOGICAL TOOL KIT

Here are suggestions for helping yourself, your child, and your child's siblings deal more effectively with the stresses and challenges of ADHD.

BE AWARE OF YOUR FEELINGS:

Raising a child with ADHD represents a large energy drain for any parent. In order to lift your child out of the quicksand of ADHD-related challenges, you must stand on solid ground. Arrange for activity to refresh and renew yourself on a regular basis. Jog, swim, go for walks, meditate, pray, go out to eat, take a bubble bath, relax in a favorite chair, flip through a magazine, or go out with friends.

Parents become frustrated with the grumpy and absentminded ADHD child in the morning, and with the power struggles and hassles surrounding bedtime. They start and end most days on a negative note with their child. One mother summarized the feelings of thousands: "Each day, I tell myself that today I will be calm and loving. By the time my child is out the door to school, I've already failed."

Seek the services of a professional counselor if you think you need help sorting out your feelings. The three most common feelings among parents of ADHD children are love, hate, and guilt: "I love him; I hate him; and I'm not a good enough parent."*

EXPAND YOUR KNOWLEDGE:

Be a helpful and instructive ally to those who supervise or assist your child. Your goal should be to know more than every professional involved with your child. Share books, tapes, videos, magazine and journal articles, and information you have learned through parent discussion programs or any other reliable source.

* For extended discussion of parents' and children's feelings in ADHD families, see *Helping Your ADD Child*, available from A.D.D. Plus.

SHARPEN YOUR PARENTING SKILLS:

Be alert to avoid the most common negative styles of parenting that occur often in ADHD families:

- **OVERINDULGENCE:** excessive shielding of the child from frustration
- **OVERPROTECTION:** excessive shielding of the child from potential danger in non-skill areas
- **INFANTILIZATION:** keeping the child ignorant, helpless, or dependent by giving too much service
- **HYPERVIGILANCE:** constant concern with the child's whereabouts, welfare, and activities
- **PITY:** excessive sympathizing after the child experiences frustration, hurt, or difficulty; exaggeration of misfortune
- **NAGGING:** excessive reminding and repeating of corrective or directive messages
- **VERBAL ABUSE:** belittling, name-calling, using sarcasm, cursing at the child *

BUILD FAMILY HARMONY:

Your children need order and routine as well as rules to guide them. They also need flexibility, affection, and emotional support from you. The best way to insure harmony in your family is to balance love and firmness.

Thank your children for little acts that might otherwise go unnoticed. Encourage them to share their success experiences at

* For extended discussion of common negative styles of parenting that occur in ADHD families, see *Positive Prescriptions for Negative Parenting,* available from A.D.D. Plus.

mealtimes and family times. Turn off the TV and pair up with each child at least once a week, doing something child-centered and recreational that involves high-quality interaction. Examples include playing sports, eating out, cooking, reading, and playing card or table games.

Decrease competition between the children in your family by changing the rules in card and table games so that the less-skilled player gets a head start and the outcome is determined more by chance. Arrange projects for the children to do together. Start with something simple, such as making a list together (main dishes your family could have, breakfast cereals to buy), then encourage more involved, cooperative endeavors, such as reorganizing or making something. Cooking together provides many opportunities for close sibling cooperation and parent-child togetherness.

Do things as a family every once in a while, even if the activity is very work-oriented. A regular family play time or family meeting works well in ADHD families. Make decisions and solve problems together, and include snacks (prepared by parent-child or sibling pairs) and distribution of allowances.

The most common complaint made by siblings of hyperactive boys is, "He gets into my room and takes my things." If violation of a sibling's living space is a problem in your family, take extra measures to provide insulation and protection. Give the sibling a separate bedroom with a lock on the door. Allow additional locks within the bedroom for the diary, dresser, or other private items. Avoid having the two children take the same dance lessons or play the same musical instrument. In general, try to avoid competition in any aspect of their daily lives.

Fairness does not mean *sameness*. It means giving each child whatever that child uniquely needs. Provide for each child whatever that child is ready to accept and use. Feel no obligation to provide identical privileges for all children. If an older sibling helps more with chores, for example, consider allowing a later bedtime and higher allowance for that child.

PREVENT PROBLEMS AT HIGH-STRESS TIMES:

- **CHORES:** The five key secrets to smoother chore times and getting more cooperation begin with **CH:**

  CHUNKS: Break down large chores into smaller ones.
  CHARTS: Use charts (not the parent's tongue) to tell children which chores are to be done and by whom.
  CHOICE: Allow the children to choose from among a few chores each day.
  CHANGE: Rotate the chore menu each month.
  CHANNELING: Don't let the chores gridlock or interlock; no child's chores should depend on another child's performance. *

- **TRAVEL**: For hassle-free travel by car or public conveyance, keep your child's hands busy with a new deck of playing cards, art or craft materials, or drawing supplies. Keep your child's mind occupied with games to play during the trip, such as "Twenty Questions," "Hangman," "I Spy," predicting license plate numbers, and travel Bingo. Take along some food to keep your child's mouth full and prevent protein depletion. In short, the keys are hands, mind, and mouth.

- **MORNINGS:** Most mornings, children with ADHD are somewhat irritable and power strugglish, or they are disorganized and absentminded. Bring out the **BEST** in the morning:

  B: Serve a protein-rich **BEDTIME** snack the night before.
  E: Give **EARLY** medication: Ask the physician to prescribe a small amount to be given 30 minutes before arising.
  S: **SET** out clothes and school supplies the night before.
  T: Practice **TRAFFIC** control. Decide in advance who sits where during breakfast.

---

* For extended discussion on how to simplify chores and reduce conflicts over routines, see *Helping Hands and Smiling Faces,* available from A.D.D. Plus.

- **BEDTIMES:** The average child takes 20 minutes to get to sleep, while children with ADHD take 40 minutes. Make everything **SEEM** better at bedtime:

  S: Take advantage of **SKIN** awareness by giving your child a back rub.
  E: Provide interesting things for the **EYES** to look at, such as glow-in-the-dark ceiling stickers or a lighted aquarium.
  E: Provide interesting things for the **EARS** to listen to, such as tape-recorded bedtime stories or music.
  M: Serve an additive-free, protein-rich bedtime snack for the **MOUTH.**

- **LEAVING FOR SCHOOL:** Put all books, lunch supplies or tickets, and notebooks in a prominent location the night before. Use a chair to block the front or back door or a basket mounted at eye level and placed next to the door. Or use a long cord to attach your child's shoes to the notebook or connect the basket to the doorknob. Have a simple checklist for remembering everything your child has to take to school.

- **RETURNING HOME FROM SCHOOL:** If your child will be unsupervised after returning home, have a written list of reminders, including when to take any needed medication. Arrange a phone call to or from you at a specified time each afternoon. Supervision by an older sibling should be limited to safety concerns, rather than bossing the child with ADHD.

USE PREVENTIVE DISCIPLINE:

Children with ADHD (hyperactive-impulsive type) tend to misbehave more than non-ADHD children. Use the **FOUR S's** to prevent discipline problems:

- **SCHEDULE** activities that meet your child's needs on a regular basis: Misbehavior reflects unmet needs. For example, build in weekly athletics and extracurricular activities to prevent boredom-based misbehavior.

- **STRUCTURE** situations by placing objects in such a way as to corral your child into correct behavior. For example, a fun-idea list taped to a door to prevent boredom-based misbehavior.

- **SUPERVISE** every so often and check on whether your child is misbehaving and whether your child's needs are being met.

- **SUPPORT** your child by helping during frustrating situations. Help during part of tasks (the beginning or the end), rather than doing tasks totally for your child.

BUILD SELF-ESTEEM:

To help with self-esteem, involve your child in activities that will build self-confidence and an *"I can do it!"* feeling. For most children with ADHD the most attractive sources of self-esteem uplift make a **MINT:**

M: Arrange activities involving rapid **MOVEMENT,** such as hockey, skateboarding, roller skating, and bicycling.
I: Arrange activities that follow from the child's **INTERESTS,** such as computers, mechanics, and sports.
N: Arrange **NONCOMPETITIVE** activities, such as martial arts, weight-lifting, swimming, bodybuilding, and bicycling.
T: Capitalize on native **TALENTS** by involving art, music, drama, or other areas in which the child has shown talent or skill.

IMPROVE SOCIAL SKILLS:

Review step by step the changes needed to improve your child's social adjustment. Use role-playing and rehearsal, or compose paragraphs describing a child using social skills, and have your child answer study questions about them.

- **ASSERTION:** If your child has trouble being a peacemaker in potential conflict situations, teach this three-part assertion statement:

1. "Please stop...(identify actions the other child is doing)"
2. "Please do...(state actions your child would like the other child to do instead.)"
3. "If you do that, I'll do...(accommodation your child will do to support the changes requested)"

▶ **TEMPTATION RESISTANCE:** Help your child resist peer pressure for mischief with these self-talk messages:

1. Stop and think: What should I do now?
2. To do well, I should slow down.
3. They are tricking me by trying to get me into trouble.
4. Make a once-and-for-all decision not to listen to them.
5. Just because they want me to do something doesn't mean I have to go along with it.

▶ **ANGER CONTROL:** Most children and teens with ADHD have difficulty handling their own anger. Consider teaching skills such as these:*

1. Transform *anger* into *effort* to solve the situation by playing the **ACE** of anger:

   A: **ADAPT** by changing your approach to solving the situation and stop frustrating yourself.
   C: **CONFRONT** the person who is frustrating or hurting you.
   E: **ESCAPE** by withdrawing from the situation if you can't solve it by playing the **A** or the **C**. Change how you deal with the people involved so they can't keep hurting you.

2. Write down concerns, or have an adult write them down. Then talk about them on a regular basis with a caring adult at home or at school.

---

* For detailed suggestions on how to train any child or adolescent in anger control, see *Anger-Control Training for Children and Teens,* available from A.D.D. Plus.

3. Rate situations for their anger level:

   GREEN LIGHT situation means, "I'm unlikely to get angry here," and I can continue without worrying about whether I will get angry.
   YELLOW LIGHT situation means, "I might get angry here," so I will tell myself to stay in control and stay calm.
   RED LIGHT situation means, "I'm starting to lose control and get into trouble," so I should stop whatever I'm doing and leave the scene temporarily.

Express the anger by jumping or running, then talk over how to solve the situation with a caring adult.

DEVELOP FRIENDSHIP SKILLS:

The most common concern expressed by children with ADHD is that they don't have enough friends. Here are 12 key friendship skills your child should know:

1. The friend goes first when playing.
2. Talk nicely about your friend.
3. The friend chooses, or you decide together, what game to play.
4. Talk about your friend's interests.
5. Take turns.
6. Show that you're happy when your friend is happy.
7. Don't be bossy.
8. Be a friendly host to your friend.
9. Say *please* and *thank you.*
10. Offer food and have kitchen fun with your friend.
11. Give small gifts and share.
12. Do small favors for your friend.

A FINAL MESSAGE OF ENCOURAGEMENT

Raising a child or teen with ADHD can be an exciting adventure in parenting. The challenges can be focal points to help you refine your skills, both as a loving supporter of your child and as an advocate for your child's needs and rights.

Keep an open mind about treatment possibilities, and remember that scientific research is a rather slow process. Just because an idea or a technique has not yet been scientifically proven doesn't mean you can't try it with your child. If it doesn't help, you will know soon enough. Obviously, you must use wise judgment in terms of the time, effort, and expense of any unproven-treatment attempt.

The most important recommendation in this booklet is to spend special time on a regular basis with your child or teen. With the right fulcrum, you can lift any weight. Keep your love bond strong, no matter what. ADHD doesn't have to ruin your child's life or the success of your family. In fact, it can often be a very positive influence. Never let the negatives outweigh the positives of the little daily successes you can experience in living with a child or teen with this condition.

THE TAYLOR HYPERACTIVITY SCREENING CHECKLIST

For each of the 21 behaviors listed below, put an X in one of the three boxes to show what is typical for the child. Rate the child's behavior when not being supervised, helped, or reminded; when not watching television or a computer screen; and when not receiving any kind of diet or medication to control behavior.

Indicate the trend. Try to avoid column B ratings. A 51% trend in either direction should merit an A or C rating. Compared with other children of approximately the same age, this child typically shows behavior:

A. MORE LIKE THIS		B. NO TREND	C. MORE LIKE THIS	
☐	QUIET PERSON	☐	NOISY AND TALKATIVE PERSON	☐
☐	VOICE VOLUME IS SOFT OR AVERAGE	☐	VOICE IS GENERALLY TOO LOUD FOR THE SITUATION	☐
☐	FEW MOUTH OR BODY NOISES	☐	MAKES LOTS OF CLICKS, WHISTLES, AND SOUNDS WITH MOUTH OR BODY	☐
☐	WALKS AT APPROPRIATE TIMES	☐	FLITS AROUND, RUNS AHEAD, NEEDS TO BE CALLED BACK, JUMPY	☐
☐	KEEPS HANDS TO SELF	☐	POKES, TOUCHES, FEELS, AND GRABS	☐
☐	APPEARS CALM, CAN BE STILL	☐	OFTEN HAS A BODY PART MOVING; FIDGETS WITH HANDS OR FEET; SQUIRMY	☐
☐	CAN JUST SIT	☐	MUST BE DOING SOMETHING TO OCCUPY SELF WHEN SITTING; QUICKLY BORED	☐
☐	SLOW TO REACT, DELIBERATE, NOT IMPULSIVE	☐	TOO QUICK TO REACT, IMPULSIVE, ENGAGES MOUTH AND MUSCLES BEFORE BRAIN	☐
☐	UNDERSTANDS WHY PARENTS/TEACHER/OTHERS ARE DISPLEASED AFTER MISBEHAVIOR	☐	FEELS PICKED ON, IS SURPRISED AND CONFUSED ABOUT WHY OTHERS ARE DISPLEASED; DOESN'T CONNECT OWN ACTIONS WITH OTHERS' REACTIONS	☐
☐	PLANS AND THINKS AHEAD TO CONSEQUENCES BEFORE ACTING; CAREFUL	☐	DOES THINGS WITHOUT CONSIDERING THE CONSEQUENCES AHEAD OF TIME; DOESN'T PLAN WELL; CARELESS	☐

☐	CONCERNED ABOUT PUNISHMENTS AND CONSEQUENCES; SUBMISSIVE	☐	PRETENDS TO HAVE AN *I DON'T CARE* ATTITUDE IF THREATENED OR PUNISHED; DEFIANT	☐
☐	AVOIDS OTHER CHILDREN'S MISCHIEF	☐	ATTRACTED OR CURIOUS ABOUT MISCHIEF; GETS INVOLVED OR STARTS IT	☐
☐	OBEYS DIRECTIONS AND FOLLOWS ORDERS	☐	DISOBEYS OR FORGETS; NEEDS SUPERVISION OR REMINDING	☐
☐	CONSTANT MOOD WITH MILD OR SLOW MOOD CHANGES; A CALM PERSON	☐	MOODY, UNPREDICTABLE, QUICK TO ANGER OR CRY	☐
☐	EASYGOING, HANDLES FRUSTRATION WITHOUT MUCH ANGER, PATIENT, CAN BE TEASED	☐	IRRITABLE, IMPATIENT, EASILY FRUSTRATED	☐
☐	EMOTIONS ARE REASONABLY CONTROLLED, ARE NOT EXTREME, AND DON'T DISRUPT RELATIONSHIPS	☐	EMOTIONS ARE EXTREME AND POORLY CONTROLLED; NO *DAMPER PEDAL* ON EMOTIONS; EXPLOSIVE; TANTRUMS	☐
☐	COOPERATES WITH, OBEYS AND ENFORCES THE RULES OF WORK AND PLAY	☐	ARGUES AND GRIPES ABOUT THE RULES; WANTS TO BE THE EXCEPTION; OPPOSITIONAL	☐
☐	GIVES UP WHEN DENIED A REQUESTED PRIVILEGE, ITEM, OR ACTIVITY	☐	BADGERS, PESTERS, PUSHES, WON'T GIVE UP OR TAKE *NO* FOR AN ANSWER	☐
☐	CONCENTRATES AND BLOCKS OUT DISTRACTIONS WHEN WORKING ON SOMETHING OF MEDIUM INTEREST, OR WHEN MENTAL DISCIPLINE IS REQUIRED	☐	EASILY DISTRACTED BY NOISES AND PEOPLE NEARBY; SHORT ATTENTION SPAN	☐
☐	FOLLOWS THROUGH; HAS AN ORGANIZED APPROACH TO ACTIVITIES; FINISHES PROJECTS	☐	FLITS FROM ACTIVITY TO ACTIVITY; STARTS THINGS WITHOUT FINISHING THEM; GETS SIDETRACKED	☐
☐	DOESN'T TRY TO BOTHER OR HURT OTHERS WITH WORDS	☐	NEEDLES, TEASES, "MOUTHY;" HAS TO HAVE THE LAST WORD	☐

The score is the total number of items in Column B plus twice the number of items in Column C. If the child's score is: 0 to 24: the ADHD syndrome (attention deficit hyperactivity disorder) is not indicated; 25 to 27: borderline; 28 to 32: mild hyperactivity; 33 to 37: moderate hyperactivity level; 38 to 42: severe hyperactivity.

THE TAYLOR SCHOOL MEDICATION EFFECTIVENESS REPORT

CHILD'S NAME ______________________________
GRADE ______ **YOUR NAME** ______________________________
PHONE ______________________________
TIME PERIOD BEING RATED:
From (date) __________________ To (date) ______________
CURRENT REGIMEN:
____mg. of __________________________taken at ______A.M./P.M.
____mg. of __________________________taken at ______A.M./P.M.

1. DESIRED EFFECTS:

If there is a difference between mornings and afternoons, give separate gradings for each half of the school day. Supplying only one grade for each effect means that the grade would be the same throughout the entire school day. Simply fill it out as you would a Grade Report, with these grades:

GRADE RATING:	PERCENT OF EXPECTED DURATION OF MEDICATION EFFECTS: (4.5 hours for short-acting) (7.5 hours for long-acting)
A Excellent-very pleasant	(80% to 100%)
B Good-OK, livable with	(60% to 80%)
C Fair-barely tolerable	(40% to 60%)
D Poor-very unpleasant	(20% to 40%)
F Failure-not tolerable	(less than 20%)

100%	80%	60%	40%	20%	0%
A	B	C	D	F	

_____ **ACTIVITY CONTROL:** Mouth, hands, and feet well controlled; sits for normal length of time; not fidgety or squirmy; doesn't poke, touch, and grab; stays seated appropriately.

_____ **BRAIN IN GEAR:** Not impulsive, asks thoughtful questions, understands and remembers clearly, not absentminded, seems "tuned in," stops and thinks before taking action.

_____ **CONSCIENCE:** Considers moral aspects of decisions; doesn't lie, cheat, or steal; respects boundaries; asks permission before doing things; repentant and apologetic if caught in a misdeed.

_____ **DILIGENCE:** Does things without being reminded or nagged, faces tasks and responsibilities head-on, wants to do a good and thorough job, earnest and serious-minded rather than flippant, careful rather than careless, concerned about neatness.

_____ **EMOTIONAL CONTROL:** Patient, can be teased, not easily upset, can take frustrations in stride, doesn't have tantrums.

_____ **FOCUSING:** Normal attention span, pursues a goal without getting sidetracked, completes activities, not overly distractible, doesn't flit from activity to activity.

_____ **GENTLENESS:** Doesn't argue or engage in power struggles, obedient, cooperative, respects authority.

_____ **HELPFULNESS:** Polite, generous, courteous, kindhearted, doesn't demand own way with other children.

A's and B's in all eight desired effects signifies correct dosage for ADD/ ADHD symptom control.

2. UNDESIRED EFFECTS:

Please indicate the levels that are happening:

0 This effect is not occurring or is so insignificant that adapting to it requires no effort.
1 This effect is mild and manageable with just a small effort that is not inconvenient.
2 This effect is moderate, causing some inconvenience, but still livable with.
3 This effect is severe, causing great inconvenience, and cannot be allowed to continue.

RATING	EFFECT
_____	Groggy, zonked, too tired
_____	Irritable, weepy shortly after taking pills
_____	Headaches
_____	Tics; jerking muscle movements
_____	Appetite decrease
_____	Stomach complaints
_____	Other: (describe) _____________________

3. OTHER CHANGES:

Please describe any other negative changes in behavior or performance since starting this particular medication arrangement, whether or not you think they might be directly related to this child's medication treatment:

____

____

Please describe any other positive changes in behavior or performance since starting this particular medication arrangement:

____

____

THE TAYLOR CLASSROOM DAILY REPORT FORM

STUDENT__________________________ **DATE**________

COMMENTS	**YES**	**NO**
BEHAVIOR—Did my child:		
arrive on time?	☐	☐
bring needed materials?	☐	☐
remain on task?	☐	☐
participate appropriately?	☐	☐
behave correctly?	☐	☐
SCHOOLWORK—Did my child:		
complete seatwork today?	☐	☐
get a homework assignment?	☐	☐
turn in homework on time?	☐	☐
HOMEWORK—Did my child:		
do homework neatly?	☐	☐
complete homework?	☐	☐
put a proper heading on homework?	☐	☐
correctly follow directions?	☐	☐

Overdue or incomplete work still out:

Homework given today:

Additional comments:

I request a telephone call from you if initialed:

__________ Teacher __________ Parent